ArtNotes

to accompany

ARTFORMS

REVISED SEVENTH EDITION

Duane Preble
Sarah Preble

revised by
Patrick Frank

PEARSON
Prentice
Hall

Upper Saddle River, New Jersey 07458

© 2004 by PEARSON EDUCATION, INC.
Upper Saddle River, New Jersey 07458

ISBN 0-13-184228-5

Printed in the United States of America

Museum credits for fine art photos can be found with the images in the text.

Contents

PART I

Art Is . . .

Notes

James Hampton. *Throne of the Third Heaven of the Nation's Millenium General Assembly.* c. 1950–1964. *(page 1)*

_____
_____
_____
_____
_____
_____
_____
_____
_____
_____
_____

Chapter One
The Nature of Art

Notes

1 Wassily Kandinsky. *Composition iv.* 1911. *(page 3)*

2 *Preparing for a Festival.* Bali. 1992. *(page 4)*

3 *The Tree of Jesse.* West facade, Chartres Cathedral. c. 1150–1170. *(page 5)*

4 *Blackfeet Parfleche.* 1885. *(page 6)*

5 *Dish.* 10th Century. East Iran. *(page 6)*

6 *Stonehenge*. Wiltshire, England. c. 2000 B.C.E. *(page 7)*

7 James Turrell. *Roden Crater*. Work in progress. 1980 to the present. *(page 8)*

8 *Wheel of Time*. Tibetan sand mandala. a. Being created. b. Completed *(page 8)*

9 Rembrandt van Rijn. *Self-portrait*. 1658. *(page 9)*

10 Yong Soon Min. *Dwelling*. 1994. *(page 9)*

11 Romare Bearden. *Prevalence of Ritual: Tidings*. 1967. *(page 10)*

12 Romare Bearden. *Rocket to the Moon.*
1971. *(page 10)*

_____

_____

_____

_____

_____

_____

_____

_____

_____

_____

13 Romare Bearden. *(page 11)*

_____

_____

_____

_____

_____

_____

_____

_____

_____

_____

_____

14 Francisco Goya. *The Disasters of War,
No. 18: Bury Them and Say Nothing.* 1818.
(page 12)

_____

_____

_____

_____

_____

_____

_____

_____

_____

_____

_____

15 Félix González-Torres. *Untitled (Death by Gun)*. 1990. a. Installation view. b. Single sheet. *(page 12)*

16 Leni Riefenstahl. *Triumph of the Will*. 1934. *(page 13)*

17 *Decorative Panel from the Alhambra*. *(page 14)*

18 Miriam Schapiro. *Heartland.* 1985.
(page 14)

_____

_____

_____

_____

_____

_____

_____

_____

_____

_____

_____

Chapter Two
Awareness, Creativity, and Communication

Notes

19 Edward Weston. *Pepper #30*. 1980. *(page 17)*

20 Leonardo da Vinci (1452–1519). *A Group of Five Grotesque Heads*. c. 1490. *(page 18)*

21 Otto Dix. *Der Krieg (Wounded Soldier).*
1924. *(page 18)*

_____

_____

_____

_____

_____

_____

_____

_____

_____

_____

_____

_____

22 Vincent van Gogh. *Skull With a Burning
Cigarette.* 1885–1886. *(page 19)*

_____

_____

_____

_____

_____

_____

_____

_____

_____

_____

_____

_____

_____

23 Jean-Michel Basquiat. *Tobacco.* 1984. *(page
19)*

_____

_____

_____

_____

_____

_____

_____

_____

_____

_____

_____

_____

24 Kojyu, age 9. *Searching for Bugs in the Park. (page 21)*

25 *First Lines.* (page 21)

26 Alana, age 2. *House. (page 21)*

27 Alana, age 3. *Grandma. (page 21)*

28 Jeff, age 3. *Hand with Line and Spots.*
(page 21)

29 Jason, almost 4. *Mother Octopus with*
Babies. (page 22)

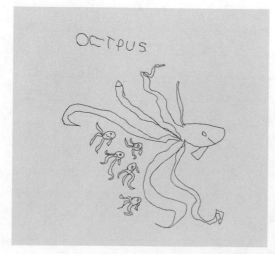

30 Yuki, age 8. *I Can Ride, I Can Ride My Unicycle. (page 22)*

31 Anonymous Child. *Birds. (page 22)*

a. This picture shows one child's drawing of a bird before exposure to coloring books.

b. Then the child colored a workbook illustration.

c. After coloring the workbook birds, the child lost creative sensitivity and self-reliance.

32 *Sanford Darling in His Kitchen. (page 23)*

33 Sabatino "Simon" Rodia. a. *Nuestro Pueblo.* Watts, California. 1921–1954. b. Detail of *Nuestro Pueblo. (page 24)*

34 James Hampton. *Throne of the Third Heaven of the Nation's Millennium General Assembly.* c. 1950–1964. *(page 25)*

35 José Rafael Aragón. *Flight Into Egypt.* c. 1850. *(page 25)*

36 William Harnett. *A Smoke Backstage.* 1877.
(page 27)

_____

_____

_____

_____

_____

_____

_____

_____

_____

_____

37 René Magritte. *La Trahison des Images
(Ceci n' est pas une pipe),* 1929. *(page 27)*

_____

_____

_____

_____

_____

_____

_____

_____

_____

38 *Chilkat Blanket.* Tlingit, before 1928.
(page 28)

_____

_____

_____

_____

_____

_____

_____

_____

_____

39 Theo van Doesburg (C.E.M. Kupper).
Abstraction of a Cow. 4 Stages. *(page 29)*

40 Nancy Graves. *Footscray,* from the
Australian Series. 1985. *(page 30)*

41 *Tukutuku Panels.* Maori peoples, New
Zealand. 1930s. *(page 30)*

42 François Auguste René Rodin. *The Kiss.*
1886. *(page 31)*

43 Constantin Brancusi. *The Kiss.* c. 1912.
(page 31)

44 *Visual Metaphor.* Student Project. *(page 32)*

45 Elliott Erwitt. *Florida.* 1968. *(page 32)*

46 Georgia O'Keeffe. *Oriental Poppies.* 1927.
(page 33)

47 Georgia O'Keeffe. *Jack-in-the-Pulpit No. V.*
1930. *(page 33)*

48 Yousuf Karsh. *Georgia O'Keeffe.* 1956.
(page 34)

49 Albrecht Dürer. *The Knight, Death and the Devil.* 1513. *(page 35)*

50 *Descent of the Ganges.* a. Overview. *(page 36)* b. Detail. *(page 37)*

51 Betye Saar. *The Liberation of Aunt Jemima.*
1972. *(page 38)*

_____
_____
_____
_____
_____
_____
_____
_____
_____
_____
_____

52 Carlos Frésquez. *Mi Casa Es Su Casa:
Yellow Wall (West).* 1997. *(page 38)*

_____
_____
_____
_____
_____
_____
_____
_____
_____
_____
_____
_____

PART TWO
The Language of Visual Experience

Notes

Claes Oldenburg and Coosje van Bruggen.
Shuttlecocks. 1994 *(page 39)*

Chapter Three
Visual Elements

53 Paul Klee. *Landscape with Yellow Birds.*
1923. *(page 40)*

54 Ansel Adams. *Rails and Jet Trails,
Roseville, California.* 1953. *(page 41)*

55 *Line Variations. (page 41)*

a. Actual line.

b. Implied line.

c. Actual straight lines and implied curved line.

d. Line created by an edge.

e. Vertical line (attitude of alert attention); horizontal line (attitude of rest).

f. Diagonal lines (slow action, fast action).

g. Sharp, jagged line.

h. Dance of curving lines.

i. Hard line, soft line.

j. Ragged, irregular line.

56 Agnes Martin. *Mountain.* c. 1960. *(page 42)*

57 Bridget Riley. *Current.* 1964. *(page 42)*

58 Jackson Pollock. *Drawing.* 1950. *(page 42)*

59 Alexander Calder (1898–1976). *Two Acrobats.* 1928. *(page 42)*

60 Duane Preble. *Blue Ginger. 1993.* (page 43)

61 Attributed to Torii Kiyonobu I. *Woman Dancer with Fan and Wand.* c. 1708. *(page 43)*

62 Torii Kiyotada (Japanese), c. 1710–1740. *An Actor of the Ichikawa Clan in a Dance Movement.* c. 1715. *(page 43)*

63 John Sloan. *The Flute Player.* 1905. *(page 43)*

64 and 64b Marc Chagall. *I and the Village.*
1911. *(page 44)*

65 A *Shape of Space.* (implied space). *(page 45)*

66 Duane Preble *Night Life* (figure-ground reversal). *(page 45)*

67 M. C. Escher. *Sky and Water I.* 1938. *(page 45)*

68 *Qennefer, Steward of the Palace.* c. 1450 B.C.E. *(page 46)*

WAS carved from hard black granite + retains the cubic blocklike appearance of quarried stone. None of the limbs projects outward into the surrounding space.

Prime example of Closed form compact mass symbolizes permanence

Symbolic container for the soul of an important person in order to insure eternal afterlife

69 Albert Giacometti. *Man Pointing.* 1947
(page 46)

_____

_____

_____

_____

_____

_____

_____

_____

_____

_____

70 Henry Moore. *Recumbent Figure.* 1938.
(page 47)

_____

_____

_____

_____

_____

_____

_____

_____

_____

_____

_____

_____

71 *Henry Moore. (page 48)*

_____

_____

_____

_____

_____

_____

_____

_____

_____

_____

_____

72 Pablo Picasso (Spanish, 1881–1973). *Head of a Young Man.* 1923. *(page 48)*

73 a. Cesar Pelli and Associates. *North Terminal Ronald Reagan Washington National Airport.* 1997. b. *Close-up Interior. (page 49)*

74 *Pond in the Garden. Wall Painting from the Tomb of Nebamun.* Egypt. c. 1400 B.C.E. *(page 50)*

75 *Clues to Spatial Depth. (page 50)*

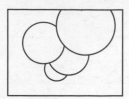

a Overlap.

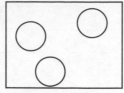

b Overlap and diminishing size.

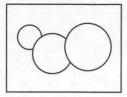

c. Vertical placement.

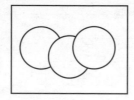

d. Overlap, vertical placement, and diminishing size.

76 Mu Qi (Japanese, d. after 1279). *Six Persimmons.* c. 1269. *(page 51)*

77 *Linear Perspective. (page 52)*

a. One-point linear perspective.

b. One-point linear perspective. Cubes above eye level, at eye level, and below eye level.

c Two-point linear perspective.

78 and 78b Raphael (Raffaello Santi)
(1483–1520). *The School of Athens.* 1508.
(page 53)

Perspective lines
showing eye level,
main vanishing point,
and left vanishing
point for the stone
block in the fore-
ground.

79 Study of Raphael's *The School of Athens.*
(page 53)

80 Asher Brown Durand. *Kindred Spirits.* 1849.
(page 54)

81 Shen Zhou, Chinese (1427–1509). *Poet on a Mountain Top (Changi–Li Yuan–T'iao)*. Series: *Landscape Album: Five Leaves* by Shen Zhou, *One Leaf* by Wen Cheng–Ming (Shen Shih–t'ien Wen Cheng-ming shan-shui-ho-chuan). Ming Dynasty, (1368–1644). *(page 55)*

82 *Isometric Perspective. (page 55)*

83 Anonymous. Detail of *Eighteen Scholars*. Song Dynasty (960–1279). *(page 55)*

84 *Wheels of the Sun Chariot. Surya Deul Temple, Konarak, India. c. 1240.* (page 56)

85 Sassetta and Workshop of Sassetta. *The Meeting of Saint Anthony and Saint Paul.* c. 1440. *(page 56)*

86 Kristin Jones and Andrew Ginzel. *Mnemonics. (page 57)*

87 Harold Edgerton. *Milk Splash Resulting from Dropping a Ball. 1936.* (page 57)

88 *Dancing Krishna.* Tanjor, Tamil Nadu. South India. Chola Dynasty. c. 1300. *(page 58)*

89 Thomas Eakins. *Man Pole Vaulting.* 1884. *(page 58)*

90 Giacomo Balla. *Dynamism of a Dog on a Leash.* 1912. *(page 59)*

91 Alexander Calder. *Big Red.* 1959. *(page 59)*

92 Daniel Chester French (1850–1931). *Abraham Lincoln,* detail of seated figure, 1922. *(page 60)*

a. As originally lit by daylight.

b. With the addition of artificial light.

93 *Dark/Light Relationships.* Value scale compared to uniform middle gray. *(page 60)*

94 *Drawing of Light on a Sphere.* Value gradations suggest light on a curving surface. *(page 61)*

95 Annibale Carracci (1560–1609). *Head of a Youth. (page 61)*

96 Michael Hayden. *Sky's the Limit.* 1987. *(page 62)*

97 *White Light Refracted by a Prism. (page 63)*

WHITE LIGHT

PRISM

RED
ORANGE
YELLOW
GREEN
BLUE
VIOLET

98 *The Three Dimensions of Color. (page 64)*

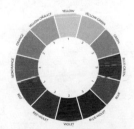

a. *Hue*—the color wheel.

b. *Value*—from light to dark.

   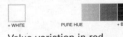

+ WHITE   PURE HUE   + BLACK

Value scale from white to black.   Value variation in red.

PURE HUE   DULLED   PURE HUE

c. *Intensity*—from bright to dull.

99 *Pigment Primaries: Subtractive Color Mixture.* (page 65)

100 *Light Primaries: Additive Color Mixture.* *(page 65)*

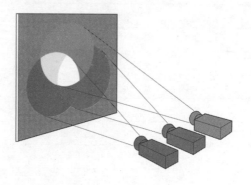

101 *Warm/Cool Colors. (page 65)*

102 *Optical Color Mixture.* Detail of Georges Seurat's (French, 1859–1891), *A Sunday on La Grande Jatte–1884,* 1884–86. *(page 66)*

103a–h Color printing detail of Sandro Botticelli's *Birth of Venus, 1486. (page 66)*

104 James Abbott McNeill Whistler. *Nocturne: Blue and Gold—Old Battersea Bridge.* 1872–1875. *(page 67)*

105 Jennifer Bartlett. *Volvo Commission.* 1984. *(page 68)*

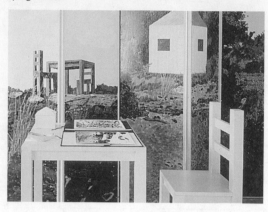

106 Keith Haring. *Untitled.* 1982. *(page 68)*

107 Meret Oppenheim. *Object (Le Dejeuner En Fourrure).* 1936. *(page 69)*

108 *Flask.* China, Tang Dynasty, 9th century.
(page 70)

_____

_____

_____

_____

_____

_____

_____

_____

_____

109 Vincent van Gogh. Detail of *Starry Night.*
1889. *(page 70)*

_____

_____

_____

_____

_____

_____

_____

110 Jan van Eyck. Detail of *Giovanni Arnolfini
and His Bride.* 1434. (See page 298.) *(page 71)*

_____

_____

_____

_____

_____

_____

_____

Chapter Four
Principles of Design

Notes

111 Jacob Lawrence. *Going Home.* 1946.
(page 73)

_____
_____
_____
_____
_____
_____
_____
_____
_____

112 Pieter de Hooch. *Interior of a Dutch House.*
1658. *(page 74)*

_____
_____
_____
_____
_____
_____
_____
_____

113 Alberto Giacometti. *Chariot.* 1950. *(page 75)*

114 James Hoban. *A Design for the President's House.* 1792. a. Elevation. b. *White House.* Front view. 1997. *(page 75)*

115 *Portrait of the Hung-Chih Emperor.* Ming Dynasty, 15th Century. *(page 76)*

116 Suzuki Haranobu. *The Evening Glow of the Ando,* from the series *Eight Parlor Views.* Edo period. 1766. *(page 77)*

117 Nicolas Poussin, French, 1594–1665. *The Holy Family on the Steps.* 1648. *(page 78)*

118 Edgar Degas (1834–1917). *Jockeys Before the Race.* c. 1878–1879. *(page 79)*

119 Beverly Pepper. *Excalibur.* San Diego
Federal Courthouse. 1975–1976. *(page 80)*

120 Francisco Goya. *Bullfight; The Agility and
Daring of Juanito Apinani.* Plate 20. *(page 81)*

121 *Luster-Painted Bowl.* Hispano-Moresque,
Manises. Spain. c. 1400. *(page 82)*

122 Raphael Sanzio. *Madonna of the Chair.*
c. 1514. *(page 83)*

123 Detail of *The Hundred Geese.* c. 1270–1300.
(page 83)

124 José Clemente Orozco. *Zapatistas.* 1931.
(page 84)

125 Claes Oldenburg (b. Sweden, 1929) and
Coosje van Bruggen (b. Netherlands 1942).
Shuttlecocks. 1994. One of four. *(page 85)*

126 *Scale Relationships. (page 85)*

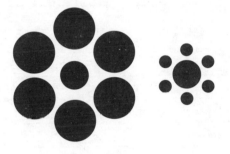

127 Rembrandt van Rijn. *Self-Portrait in a Cap,
Open Mouthed and Staring*. 1630. *(page 85)*

128 Michelangelo Buonarroti. *Pietà.* 1501.
(page 86)

129 Master of the Beautiful Madonna. *Pietà.*
c. 1415. *(page 87)*

130 Henri Matisse. Photographs of three states
of *Large Reclining Nude.* a. State I, May 3,
1935. b. State IX, May 29, 1935. c. State XII,
September 4, 1935. *(page 88)*

131 Henri Matisse (French, 1869–1954). *Large Reclining Nude. (page 89)*

132 Henri Matisse. *Self-Portrait, Three-Quarter View.* 1948. *(page 90)*

Chapter Five
Style

Notes

133 *Spirit Spouse.* Côte D'Ivoire. Baule Culture, early 20th Century. *(page 91)*

134 *Standing Parvati.* Chola Dynasty, c. 900. *(page 92)*

135 Paul Gauguin. *Self-Portrait with Halo.*
1889. *(page 93)*

_____

_____

_____

_____

_____

_____

_____

_____

_____

136 Victor Horta. *Staircase, Tassel House,
Brussels.* 1892–1893. *(page 94)*

_____

_____

_____

_____

_____

_____

_____

_____

_____

_____

137 Henry van de Velde. *Candelabrum.* c. 1902.
(page 94)

_____

_____

_____

_____

_____

_____

_____

_____

_____

_____

_____

138 Alphonse Mucha. *Cycles Perfecta.* Poster.
c. 1900. *(page 94)*

_____

_____

_____

_____

_____

_____

_____

_____

_____

_____

139 *Jar.* Ácoma Pueblo. c. 1850–1900. *(page 95)*

_____

_____

_____

_____

_____

_____

_____

_____

_____

_____

140 *Water Jar.* Zuni Pueblo. c. 1882. *(page 96)*

_____

_____

_____

_____

_____

_____

_____

_____

_____

_____

141 María and Julian Martínez. *Black on Black Storage Jar.* c. 1942. *(page 96)*

142 Claude Monet (1840–1926). *Bathers at la Grenouillère.* 1859. *(page 97)*

143 Pierre-Auguste Renoir. *Le Moulin de la Galette, Montmarte.* 1876. *(page 98)*

144 Käthe Kollwitz. *The Prisoners.* 1908.
(page 99)

145 Käthe Kollwitz. *Death Seizing a Woman.*
1934. Plate IV from the series *Death* (1934–1936).
(page 100)

146 Käthe Kollwitz (German, 1867–1945).
Self-Portrait. 1934. *(page 101)*

147 Louise Nevelson. Detail of *Shadows and Flags.* Louise Nevelson Plaza, New York. 1977–1978. *(page 102)*

148 *Louise Nevelson. (page 103)*

Chapter Six
Evaluation and Criticism

Notes

149 James Thurber. *(page 105)*

150 Dawn Marie Jingagian. *Shy Glance.* 1976.
(page 105)

151 Henri Matisse (1869–1954). *La Desserte.*
1897. *(page 106)*

_____
_____
_____
_____
_____
_____
_____
_____
_____
_____

152 Henri Matisse (1869–1954). *Harmony in
Red.* 1908–1909. *(page 106)*

_____
_____
_____
_____
_____
_____
_____
_____
_____
_____
_____
_____

153 *Robert Hughes. (page 109)*

_____
_____
_____
_____
_____
_____
_____
_____
_____
_____
_____
_____

154 Frank Modell. *(page 110)*

_____

_____

_____

_____

_____

_____

_____

_____

_____

_____

_____

PART THREE
Two-Dimensional Arts

Winslow Homer. *Sloop, Nassau.* 1899.
(page 111)

Notes

_____

_____

_____

_____

_____

_____

_____

_____

_____

_____

Chapter Seven
Drawing

155 Pamela Davis. *Carol.* 1973. *(page 112)*

156 Leonardo da Vinci. *Three Seated Figures and Studies of Machinery.* c. 1490. *(page 113)*

157 Iris Chamberlain, age 8. *Designs for Inventions.* 1992. *(page 113)*

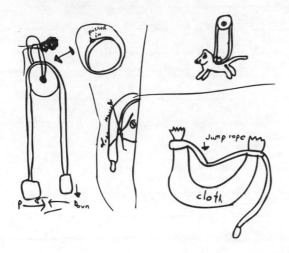

158 Frederick Franck. *Pencil Drawing* from his book *The Zen of Seeing.* *(page 113)*

159 Gerardo Campos, September 2, 1973 (left). Gerardo Campos, November 10, 1973 (right). *(page 114)*

160 Elizabeth Layton (1909–1993). *The Eyes of the Law*. 1985. *(page 114)*

161 David Hockney. *Celia in a Black Dress with White Flowers*. 1972. *(page 115)*

162 Vincent van Gogh. *Carpenter*. c. 1880. *(page 116)*

Notes

163 Vincent van Gogh. *Old Man with His Head in His Hands.* 1882. *(page 116)*

164 Vincent van Gogh. *Self Portrait with Gray Hat.* 1887. *(page 117)*

165 Michelangelo Buonarotti. Studies for the *Libyan Sibyl* on the Sistine Chapel ceiling. c. 1508. *(page 118)*

166 Pablo Picasso (1881–1973). *Guernica.*
1937. *(page 119)*

167 Pablo Picasso. *First Composition Study for
Guernica.* May 1, 1937. *(page 119)*

168 Pablo Picasso. *Composition Study for
Guernica.* May 9, 1937. *(page 119)*

169 *Types of Hatching. (page 120)*

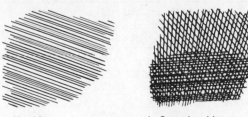

a. Hatching.   b. Cross-hatching.

c. Contour hatching.

170 Charles White. *Preacher.* 1952. *(page 120)*

171 *Drawing Tools and Their Characteristic Lines. (page 121)*

172 Judith Murray. *Obsidian*. 1988. *(page 121)*

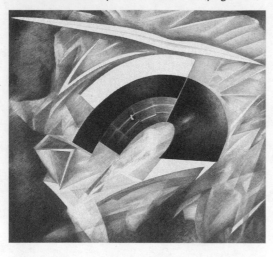

173 Georgia O'Keeffe. *Banana Flower.* 1933. *(page 122)*

174 Georges Pierre Seurat (French, 1859–1891). *L'echo, Study for Une Baignade, Asnieres.* 1882–1891. *(page 122)*

175 Rosalba Carriera. *Allegory of Painting.* c. 1720. *(page 123)*

176 Edgar Degas (1834–1917). *Le Petit Dejeuner Apres Le Bain (Jeune Femmme S'essuyant). c. 1894.* (page 123)

177 Vincent van Gogh. *The Fountain in the Hospital Garden.* 1889. *(page 124)*

178 Hokusai. *Tuning the Samisen.* c. 1820–1825.
(page 125)

179 Rembrandt van Rijn. *Saskia Asleep.* c. 1642.
(page 125)

Chapter Eight
Painting

180 Gerhard Richter. *Abstract Painting (551-4).*
1984. *(page 127)*

181 Winslow Homer (1836–1910). *Sloop,*
Nassau. 1899. *(page 128)*

182 Huang Gongwang. *Dwelling in the Fuchun Mountains.* Section of a handscroll. Yuan Dynasty. 1350. *(page 129)*

183 Fra Filippo Lippi. *Madonna and Child.* c. 1440–1445. *(page 130)*

184 Jan van Eyck. *Madonna and Child with the Chancellor Rolin.* c. 1433–1434. *(page 131)*

185 Rembrandt van Rijn. Detail of *Self-Portrait*. 1663. *(page 132)*

186 Frank Auerbach. *Head of Michael Podro*. 1981. *(page 132)*

187 Grace Hartigan. *City Life*. 1956. *(page 133)*

188 Joan Mitchell. *Border.* 1989. *(page 133)*

_____
_____
_____
_____
_____
_____
_____
_____
_____
_____
_____

189 David Hockney. *A Bigger Splash.* 1967.
(page 134)

_____
_____
_____
_____
_____
_____
_____
_____
_____
_____
_____

190 Audrey Flack. *Wheel of Fortune.* 1977–1978.
(page 134)

_____
_____
_____
_____
_____
_____
_____
_____
_____
_____

191 *Portrait of a Boy.* From Fayum, Lower
Egypt. Ca. 50–100 C.E. *(page 135)*

192 Diego Rivera. Detail from *Sugar Cane.*
1931. *(page 135)*

193 Diego Rivera. *Sugar Cane.* 1931.
(page 136)

194 Judy Baca, director; Isabel Castro, designer. *Great Wall of Los Angeles, Immigrant California.* 1976–1983. a. *1900 Immigrant California. (page 137)* b. *Jewish Arts and Science.* c. *Chinese Immigrants and Their Role in Building the Railroads. (page 138)*

Chapter Nine
Printmaking

195 Section of *The Diamond Sutra.* Chinese
Buddhist text 868. *(page 140)*

196 Katsushika Hokusai (1760–1849). *The
Wave.* c. 1830. *(page 141)*

197 Emil Nolde (German, 1867–1956). *Prophet.*
1912. *(page 141)*

_____

_____

_____

_____

_____

_____

_____

_____

_____

_____

198 Elizabeth Catlett (Mexican, 1919).
Sharecropper. 1970. *(page 142)*

_____

_____

_____

_____

_____

_____

_____

_____

_____

_____

_____

199 *Relief. (page 142)*

_____

_____

_____

_____

_____

_____

_____

_____

_____

_____

_____

200 *Intaglio. (page 142)*

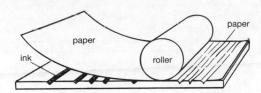

201 Albrecht Dürer (1471–1528). *The Knight, Death and the Devil.* 1513. *(page 143)*

202 Berthe Morisot (French, 1841–1985). *Little Girl with Cat.* 1888–90. *(page 144)*

203 *Drypoint Plate. (page 144)*

ink

204 Rembrandt Harmensz van Rijn (1606–1669).
Christ Preaching. c. 1652. *(page 145)*

205 Kitagawa Utamaro. *A Competitive Showing of Beauties: Hinzauru of the Heizetsuro.* c. 1796. *(page 146)*

206 Mary Cassatt. *The Letter.* 1891. *(page 146)*

207 Honoré Daumier (French, 1808–1879). *Rue Transnonain*, April 15, 1834. *(page 147)*

208 *Lithography. (page 147)*

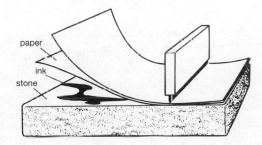

paper
ink
stone

Notes

209 Henri de Toulouse-Lautrec. *Jane Avril.*
c. 1893. *(page 148)*

210 Henri de Toulouse-Lautrec. *Jane Avril
Dansant.* c. 1893. *(page 148)*

211 Henri de Toulouse-Lautrec. *Jane Avril.
Jardin de Paris.* c. 1893. *(page 149)*

212 Andy Warhol (1928–1987).*Little Race Riot.*
1964. *(page 150)*

213 Allyn Bromley. *Greenhouse Series: Protea.*
1987. *(page 150)*

214 *Screenprinting. (page 150)*

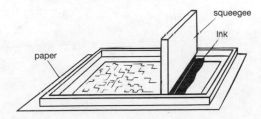

215 Willie Cole. *Stowage.* 1997. *(page 151)*

216 Alicia Candiani. *No Te Salves Ahora
[Do Not Save Yourself Now].* 1998. *(page 151)*

Chapter Ten
Camera Arts
and Computer Imaging

Notes

217 *Evolution of the Camera Obscura, Predecessor of the Modern Camera.* a. Sixteenth-century camera obscura. b. Seventeenth-century portable camera obscura. c. Seventeenth–nineteenth-century table model camera obscura. *(page 154)*

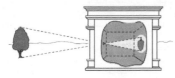

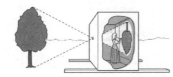

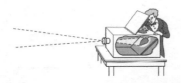

218 Louis Jacques Mandé Daguerre. *Le Boulevard du Temple.* 1839. *(page 155)*

219 Julia Margaret Cameron. *Julia Jackson.*
March 1866. *(page 156)*

220 *Human Eye and Camera.* (page 157)

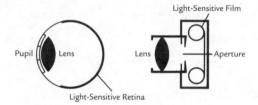

221 *Pupil of Eye and Camera Lens Aperture.*
(page 157)

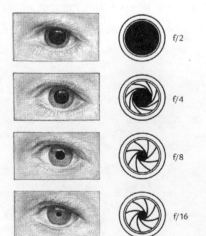

222 *Depth of Field with Aperture Adjustments.*
(page 157)

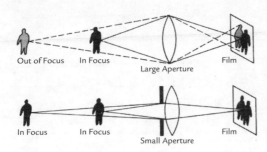

223 *Angle of View.* a. Wide-angle lens.
b. Normal lens. c. Telephoto lens. *(page 158)*

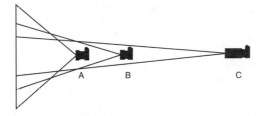

224 *Photographs of Waikiki and Diamond
Head.* a. With a wide-angle (24 mm) lens. b.
With a telephoto (135 mm) lens. *(page 158)*

225 Alfred Stieglitz. *The Flatiron Building.*
1903. *(page 159)*

226 Henri Cartier-Bresson. *Behind the Gare St.
Lazare, Paris.* 1932. *(page 159)*

227 Gyorgy Kepes (American, b. 1906).
Photogram. 1939. *(page 160)*

228 Lewis Hine. *Coal Breakers, Pennsylvania.*
1910. *(page 160)*

229 Margaret Bourke-White. *Louisville Flood
Victims.* 1937. *(page 161)*

230 Margaret Bourke-White. *Fort Peck Dam.*
First *Life* Magazine cover, November 23, 1936.
(page 161)

231 *Margaret Bourke-White Atop the Chrysler Building.* 1934. *(page 162)*

_____

_____

_____

_____

_____

_____

_____

_____

_____

_____

_____

232 Ansel Adams. *Clearing Winter Storm, Yosemite National Park, California.* 1944. *(page 163)*

_____

_____

_____

_____

_____

_____

_____

_____

_____

_____

_____

_____

_____

233 Eliot Porter. *Pool in a Brook, Pond Brook, New Hampshire, 1953. (page 164)*

_____

_____

_____

_____

_____

_____

_____

_____

_____

_____

_____

234 Jerry Uelsmann. *Untitled.* 1969. *(page 165)*

235 Sonia Landy Sheridan. *Flowers.* 1976. *(page 165)*

236 Thomas Edison and W. K. Dickson. *Fred Ott's Sneeze.* 1889. *(page 166)*

237 Eadweard Muybridge. *Galloping Horse.*
1878. *(page 166)*

238 Edwin S. Porter. *The Great Train Robbery.*
1903. *(page 167)*

239 D. W. Griffith. *Intolerance.* 1916. a. Close-up
("Little Dear One"). b. Longshot (Belshazzar's
Feast). *(page 168)*

240 Sergei Eisenstein. *The Battleship Potemkin*. 1925. *(page 169)*

241 Charlie Chaplin. *City Lights*. 1931. *(page 170)*

242 Orson Welles. *Citizen Kane*. 1941. *(page 170)*

243 Federico Fellini. *La Dolce Vita.* 1961. *(page 171)*

_____

_____

_____

_____

_____

_____

_____

_____

_____

_____

_____

_____

244 Walt Disney. *Fantasia.* 1940. *(page 172)*

_____

_____

_____

_____

_____

_____

_____

_____

_____

_____

_____

_____

_____

245 Victor Petrov. *The Old Man and the Sea.* 1940. a. Still from the film. b. The artist and the storyboard. *(page 173)*

_____

_____

_____

_____

_____

_____

_____

_____

_____

_____

246 Ridley Scott. *Blade Runner.* 1982/1993. *(page 174)*

247 Still from *Dinosaur. (page 175)*

248 Nam June Paik and John Godfrey. *Global Groove. (page 176)*

249 Joan Jonas. *Volcano Saga.* 1987. *(page 176)*

250 Dara Birnbaum. *Hostage.* 1994. *(page 177)*

251 Vera Molnar. *Parcours: Maquette For an Architectural Environment).* 1976. *(page 178)*

252 Joseph Nechtaval. *The Informed Man.*
1986. *(page 178)*

253 Camilla Benolirao Griggers. *Alienations of
the Mother Tongue.* 1996. *(page 179)*

254 William Latham. *CR3Z72. (page 179)*

255 George Legrady. Screen shot from *An Anecdoted Archive from the Cold War.* 1994. *(page 180)*

256 Annette Weintraub. Screen shot from *Sampling Broadway.* 2000 Interactive WWW work. *(page 180)*

257 James Johnson. *One Thousand Words.* 1998. Interactive www work. Screen shot from *Ikwords*, 1998. *(page 181)*

Chapter Eleven
Graphic Design and Illustration

258 Aleksandr Rodchenko and Vladimir Maiakovskii. *Give Me Sun at Night.* Design for Poster, 1923. *(page 183)*

259 Cassandre (Adolpe Jean-Marie Moreall). *L'atlantique*, 1932. *(page 184)*

260 Eric Rodenbeck. *The Empty City.* 1999.
(page 184)

261 Henry Dreyfuss. *Symbols.* 1972. *(page 185)*

a. hotel   b. stop   c. drinking fountain

d. restaurant   or   or

262 *Olympic Pictograms—Downhill Skiing.* a. 1976.
b. 1988. c. 1992. d. 1994. e. 1998. *(page 185)*

263 1996 *Summer Games. (page 185)*

264 *Symbol for a Coffee House.* Esienberg
and Associates, Dallas, Texas. Arthur Eisenberg,
creative director; Bruce Wynne-Jones, art
director/designer/illustrator. *(page 186)*

265 *NASA Letterhead Stationery.* a. 1959. Logo
designer. c.1959 James Modarelli (US). b. 1974.
Designers Danne & Blackburn, NYC. 1973 c. 1992.
Logo designer James Modarelli (US). *(page 186)*

266 Herb Lubalin, assisted by Alan Peckolick and Tom Carnase. *Mother & Child*, logo for a magazine (never produced). 1965. *(page 187)*

267 Tobias Frere-Jones. *Three Typefaces: Nobel™, Armada™, Garage Gothic™*. 1992–1994. *(page 187)*

268 *Three Invented Typefaces. Roughhouse, Crackhouse, Housemaid*. Designers (from top): Andy Cruz, Jeremy Dean, Kristen Faulker. 1992–1994. *(page 187)*

269 *Silence=Death.* 1986. *(page 188)*

270 *North American Tour '94. (page 188)*

271. Scott Osman. *Tropi-Nasa Premium Rave Flyer. (page 189)*

272 Kristin and Lanny Sommese. *Self-Promotion Poster*. Sommese Design. *(page 189)*

273 *Newspaper Advertisement*. Creative Direction: Larry Tolpin, Stephen Creet, Michael McLaughlin. BBDO Canada. 1998. *(page 189)*

274 *Lost in the Stars: The Music of Kurt Weill*. 1985. *(page 190)*

275 David Carson. *Pages from Ray Gun Magazine.* 1993. *(page 190)*

276 José Guadalupe Posada (Mexican, 1852–1913). *Las Bravísimas Calaveras Guatemaltecas de Mora de Morales.* 1907. *(page 191)*

277 Norman Rockwell. *Museum Worker.* Cover for *Saturday Evening Post,* March 2, 1946. *(page 191)*

278 Maurice Sendak. *Reading is Fun.* Poster.
(page 192)

_____

_____

_____

_____

_____

_____

_____

_____

_____

_____

_____

_____

PART FOUR
Three-Dimensional Arts

Notes

Ken Smith and Jim Conti. *Glowing Topiary Garden*. Liberty Plaza, New York City 1997–1998. *(page 193)*

Chapter Twelve
Sculpture

Notes

279 Alexander Calder. *Obus.* 1972. *(page 194)*

280 *Apollo.* c. 415 B.C.E. *(page 194)*

106

281 *Army on the March.* Angkor Wat, The
Great Temple of the Khmers, Cambodia.
Sandstone. *(page 195)*

282 Robert Longo. Middle portion, *Corporate
Wars: Wall of Influence.* 1982. *(page 195)*

283 *Double Figure, Man and Female.* Mexican.
c. 700 A.D. *(page 196)*

284 Robert Arneson. *California Artist.* 1982.
(page 196)

_____

_____

_____

_____

_____

_____

_____

_____

_____

_____

285 Scott Chamberlin. *Ahyre.* 1998. *(page 197)*

_____

_____

_____

_____

_____

_____

_____

_____

_____

_____

_____

286 Duane Hanson (American, 1925–1996).
Museum Guard. 1975. *(page 198)*

_____

_____

_____

_____

_____

_____

_____

_____

_____

_____

287 Charles Ray. *Self-Portrait*. 1990.
(page 198)

288 Rachel Whiteread. *Public Art Fund
Watertower Project*. 1997. *(page 199)*

289 Michelangelo Buonarroti. *Awakening
Slave*. 1530–1534. *(page 200)*

290 *Massive Stone Head.* Possibly representing a planetary deity 12th–10th centuries B.C.E. *(page 200)*

291 Elizabeth Catlett. *Mother and Child #2.* 1971. *(page 201)*

292 *Kwan Yin. Bodhisattva.* China, 13th–14th century *(page 201)*

293 Julio González. *Maternity.* 1934.
(page 202)

294 Julio González. *The Montserrat.* 1936–1937.
(page 202)

295 Deborah Butterfield. *Nahele.* 1986.
(page 203)

296 Pablo Picasso. *Bull's Head.* 1943.
(page 204)

297 Pablo Picasso. *Baboon and Young.* 1951.
(page 204)

298 Alexander Calder. *Untitled.* 1976.
(page 205)

299 *Alexander Calder with His Circus.* 1929.
(page 206)

300 Cai Guo Qiang. *Borrowing Your Enemy's
Arrows.* 1998. *(page 207)*

301 Bessie Harvey. *Snake Through Eye.* 1989.
(page 207)

302 Marisol (b. 1930). *Women and Dog.* 1964. *(page 208)*

303 Nam June Paik. *Internet Dweller: wol.five.ydpb.* 1994. *(page 209)*

304 Ilya Kabakov. *The Man Who Flew Into Space from His Apartment.* From *Ten Characters.* 1981–1988. *(page 209)*

305 a-b-c. James Turrell. *Meeting.* 1980–1986.
(page 210)

306 Mel Chin. *Revival Field.* Pig's Eye Landfill,
St. Paul, Minnesota. 1993. *(page 210)*

Chapter Thirteen
Clay, Glass, Metal, Wood, Fiber

Notes

307 Miriam Schapiro. *Personal Appearance #3.* 1973. *(page 212)*

308 *Tea Bowl.* Satsuma ware. 17th century. *(page 214)*

309 Kakiemon V. *Bell-Flower-Shaped Bowl.*
17th century. *(page 214)*

310 *Nampeyo Decorating Pottery.* 1901.
(page 215)

311 Nampeyo. *Canteen.* c. 1880. *(page 215)*

312 Nampeyo. *Seed Jar.* c. 1915–1916.
(page 216)

313 Peter Voulkos. *Gallas Rock.* 1960.
(page 217)

314 Toshiko Takaezu. *Ceramic Forms.* 1986.
(page 217)

315 Kreg Kallenberger. *Full Moon in Curtin Canyon.* 1997. *(page 219)*

316 Dale Chihuly. *Mauve Seaform Set with Black Lip Wraps* from the *"Seaforms"* Series. 1985. *(page 219)*

317 *D'arenberg Basin.* Syria. 13th century. *(page 220)*

318 Mark Pierce. *Earrings.* 1982. *(page 220)*

319 Albert Raymond Paley (b. 1944). *Portal Gates.* 1974. *(page 221)*

320 Virginia Dotson. *Cross Winds.* 1989. *(page 222)*

321 Sam Maloof. *Double Rocking Chair.* 1992.
(page 222)

322 *The Ardabil Carpet.* Tabriz. 1540.
(page 223)

323 Diane Itter. *Pattern Scape.* 1985.
(page 224)

324 Pieced by Rosie Lee Tompkins; restruc-
tured and quilted by Willia Ette Graham.
String. 1985. *(page 224)*

325 Polly Apfelbaum. *L'Avventura.* 1994. *(page
225)*

326 Olga de Amaral. *Gold Mountain.* 1992.
(page 225)

327 Faith Ringgold *Mrs. Jones and Family.*
1973. *(page 226)*

328 Magdalena Abakanowicz. *Backs (in
Landscape).* 1976–1982. *(page 226)*

329 Faith Ringgold. *Tar Beach.* 1988. *(page 227)*

330 Faith Ringgold. With detail of *The Purple Quilt*. 1986. *(page 228)*

Chapter Fourteen
Architecture and Environmental Design

331 Margaret Courtney-Clarke. *Beautifying the Space in Which We Live Makes Life More Bearable.* From *African Canvas*, Namibia, Africa. 1990. *(page 229)*

332 *Dolmen.* Crocuno, north of Carnac, France. *(page 230)*

333 *Great Zimbabwe.* Zimbabwe. Before 1450.
a. Plan. b. Interior. *(page 231)*

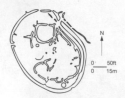

334 *Post-and-Beam Construction.* (page 232)

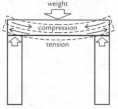

335 *Colonnade, Court of Amenhotep III.* Temple of
Amun-Mut-Khonsu. View of the great court with
double row of papyrus-clustered columns. 18th
dynasty. Luxor, Thebes, Egypt. c. 1390 B.C.E. *(page 232)*

336 *Round Arch. (page 233)*

keystone

_____
_____
_____
_____
_____
_____
_____
_____
_____
_____

337 *Barrel Vault. (page 233)*

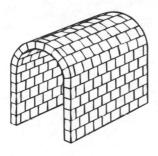

_____
_____
_____
_____
_____
_____
_____
_____
_____
_____
_____
_____

338 *Groin Vault. (page 233)*

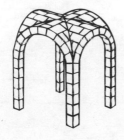

_____
_____
_____
_____
_____
_____
_____
_____
_____
_____
_____

339 *Arcarde. (page 233)*

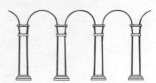

340 *Pont Du Gard.* Nimes, France. 15 C.E.
(page 233)

341 *Dome.* a. Dome (arch rotated 180º).
b. Dome on a cylinder. c. Dome on pendentives.
(page 234)

342 *Hagia Sophia.* 532–535. a. Exterior.
b. Interior. *(page 234)*

343 *Notre Dame de Chartres.* Chartres, France.
1145–1513. *(page 235)*

344 *Gothic Arch. (page 235)*

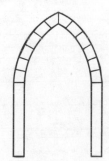

345 *Flying Buttresses. (page 235)*

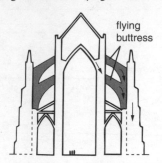

flying
buttress

346 *Trusses. (page 236)*

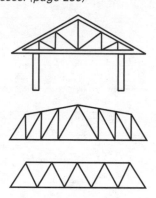

347 *Balloon Frame. (page 236)*

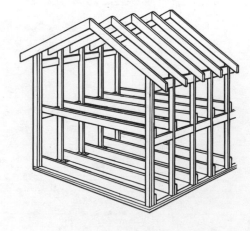

348 Joseph Paxton. *Crystal Palace*. London.
1850–1851. (damaged by fire in 1935).
a. Exterior. b. Interior. *(page 237)*

349 Gustave Eiffel. *Eiffel Tower*. Paris. 1889.
(page 238)

350 Louis Sullivan. *Wainwright Building*. St.
Louis, Missouri. 1890–1891. *(page 239)*

351 Le Corbusier. *Domino Construction System.* 1914–1915. *(page 240)*

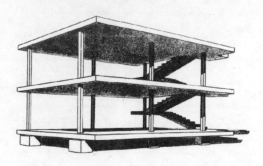

352 Walter Gropius. *Bauhaus.* Dessau, Germany. 1925–1926. *(page 240)*

353 *Steel-Frame Construction.* (page 241)

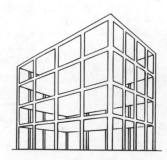

354 Ludwig Mies van der Rohe and Philip Johnson. *Seagram Building.* New York. 1956–1958. *(page 241)*

355 *Suspension Structures.* a. Exterior, natatorium. b. Interior, natatorium. c. Aerial view. *(page 242)*

356 Kenzo Tange. *Olympic Stadiums (Yoyogi Sports Center).* Tokyo, Japan. 1964. *(page 242)*

357 Eero Soarinen. *Shell Structure (TWA Terminal).* Kennedy Airport, N.Y. 1956–1962. *(page 243)*

358 *Folded Plate Roof. (page 243)*

359 *Pneumatic Structure. (page 243)*

higher air pressure inside supports
the flexible structure

360 *Jeppesen Terminal Building.* Denver
International Airport. 1994. *(page 243)*

361 Gae Aulenti. *Italian Pavilion.* Expo '92,
Seville, Spain. *(page 244)*

362 Gae Aulenti. *Musée d'orsay.* Paris, France.
1986. *(page 244)*

363 Zaha Hadid. *(page 245)*

364 Zaha Hadid. *Melbury Court Apartment.* London. 1985. *(page 245)*

365 Zaha Hadid. *Vitra Fire Station.* Vitra Furniture Company, Weil-am-Rhein, Germany. 1993. *(page 245)*

366 Frank O. Gehry. *Guggenheim Museum Bilbao.* Bilbao, Spain. 1997. a. Interior. b. Exterior. *(page 246)*

367 Mick Pearce. *The Eastgate Complex.* Harare, Zimbabwe. 1996. a. Exterior. b. Energy use. *(page 247)*

368 Frank Lloyd Wright. *Falling Water (Edgar Kaufmann Residence).* Bear Run, Pennsylvania. 1936. *(page 248)*

369 *Frank Lloyd Wright.* 1936. *(page 249)*

370 Henry Hobson Richardson. *Trinity Church.* 1877. I. M. Pei and Partners. *John Hancock Tower.* 1974. Copley Square, Boston. *(page 250)*

371 Ken Smith and Jim Conti. *Glowing Topiary Garden.* Liberty Plaza, New York. 1997–1998. *(page 251)*

PART FIVE
Art as Cultural Heritage

Notes

Wu Chen. *Album Leaf* from *Manual of Ink Bamboo.* 1350. *(page 253)*

_____

_____

_____

_____

_____

_____

_____

_____

_____

_____

Chapter Fifteen
Prehistoric to Early Civilization

372 *Venus of Willendorf.* c. 25,000–20,000 B.C.E. *(page 255)*

373 *Venus de Lespugue.* a. back view b. front view *(page 255)*

374 *Great Hall of Bulls, Left-Hand Wall.*
Lascaux Cave, Dordogne, France.
c. 15,000–10,000 B.C.E. *(page 256)*

375 *Wall Painting of Animals.* Chauvet Cave,
Pont d'Arc, France. C. 28,000 B.C.E. *(page 256)*

376 *Deer and Hands.* Las Manos Cave,
Argentina. c. 15,000 B.C.E. *(page 257)*

377 *Earthenware Beaker.* Susa, Iran. c. 4000
B.C.E. *(page 258)*

378 *Burial Urn.* Kansu type. Chinese, Neolithic
period. c. 2200 B.C.E. *(page 259)*

379 *An Evolution of Abstraction.* From
Neolithic pottery, Shensi Province, China.
(page 259)

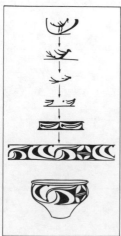

380 *Pictographs to Writing East and West.*
(page 260)

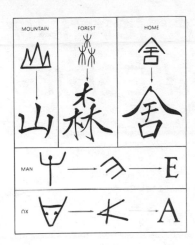

381 *Earliest Centers of Civilization, 3500–1500
B.C.E. (page 260)*

Chapter Sixteen

Ancient through Medieval in the Middle East and Europe

382 *Ziggurat of Ur-Nammu.* Iraq. c. 2100 B.C.E.
a. Reconstruction drawing. b. Incomplete
restoration. *(page 261)*

383 Reconstructed *Lyre.* From "The King's
Grave" tomb RT 789, Ur. c. 2650–2550 B.C.E.
(page 262)

384 *Head of an Akkadian Ruler.* Nineveh.
c. 2300–2200 B.C.E. *(page 262)*

385 *The Great Pyramids.* Giza, Egypt. Pyramid of
Mycerinus, c. 2500 B.C.E.; Pyramid of Chefren, 2650
B.C.E.; Pyramid of Cheops, c. 2570 B.C.E. *(page 263)*

386 *The Ancient Middle East. (page 263)*

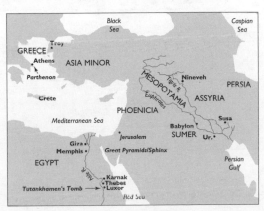

387 *Funerary Temple of Queen Hatshepsut.*
Deir el-Bahari. c. 1490–1460 B.C.E. *(page 264)*

388 *King Mycerinus and Queen Khamerernebty.*
Egypt, Giza, Old Kingdom, Dynasty 4, reign of
Mycerinus, 2532–2510 B.C.E. *(page 264)*

389 *Mask from Mummy Case.* Tutankhamen. c.
1340 B.C.E. *(page 265)*

390 *Wall Painting from the Tomb of Nebamun.*
Thebes, Egypt. c. 1450 B.C.E. *(page 265)*

_____

_____

_____

_____

_____

_____

_____

_____

_____

391 Exekias. *Greek Vase.* Achilles and Ajax
playing draughts. c. 540 B.C.E. *(page 266)*

_____

_____

_____

_____

_____

_____

_____

_____

_____

_____

392 *Kouros.* Statue of a youth. c. 610–600 B.C.E.
(page 266)

_____

_____

_____

_____

_____

_____

_____

_____

_____

_____

393 *Warrior.* 5th century B.C.E. *(page 267)*

394 Ictinus and Callicrates. *Parthenon.* Acropolis, Athens. 448–432 B.C.E. a. View from the north-west. b. View from the southwest. *(page 268)* c. *Parthenon Frieze.* Poseidon, Apollo, and Artemis. *(page 269)*

395 *Architectural Orders. (page 269)*

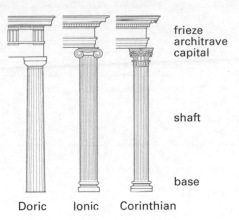

frieze
architrave
capital

shaft

base

Doric   Ionic   Corinthian

396 *Venus De Medici.* 3rd century B.C.E. *(page 270)*

397 *The Laocoön Group.* Roman copy of a 1st-
or 2nd-century B.C.E. Greek original, perhaps
after Agesander, Athenodorus, and Polydorus of
Rhodes. c. 1st century C.E. *(page 271)*

398 *Female Portrait.* c. 54–117 C.E. *(page 271)*

399 *Pantheon.* Rome. 118–125 C.E. a. View of entrance. b` Plan. c` Section. *(page 272)*

400 Giovanni Paolo Panini (Roman, 1691–1765). *The Interior of the Pantheon, Rome.* c. 1734. *(page 272)*

401 *Europe from 117 to 1400.* (page 273)

402 *Roman Painting.* Detail of west wall in a villa at Boscoreale. 1st century B.C.E. *(page 273)*

403 *Christ Teaching His Disciples.* Catacomb of Domitilla, Rome. Mid-4th century C.E. *(page 274)*

404 *Head of Constantine.* c. 312 C.E. *(page 274)*

405 *Old St. Peter's Basilica.* Rome. C. 320–335.
a. Reconstruction drawing. b. Interior view of
basilica of Saint Peter's. c. Plan. *(page 275)*

406a-b *San Vitale.* Ravenna, Italy. 526–547. a.
Exterior. b. Plan. *(page 276)*

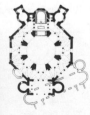

406c-d c. *Empress Theodora*. d. Interior. *(page 277)*

_____

_____

_____

_____

_____

_____

_____

_____

_____

_____

407 *Christ as Pantocrator with Mary and Saints.* Apse mosaic. Cathedral of Monreale, Sicily. Late 12th century. *(page 278)*

_____

_____

_____

_____

_____

_____

_____

_____

_____

_____

408 Andrei Rublev. *Old Testament Trinity.* c. 1410–1420. *(page 279)*

_____

_____

_____

_____

_____

_____

_____

_____

409 Byzantine School. *Madonna and Child on a Curved Throne*. Byzantine, 13th century. *(page 279)*

410 *Scythian Animal.* 5th century B.C.E. *(page 280)*

411 *Purse Cover.* From the Sutton Hoo Ship Burial, Suffolk, England. Before 655. *(page 280)*

412 *Chi-Rho Monogram (XP).* Page from the *Book of Kells.* Late 8th century. *(page 281)*

_____

_____

_____

_____

_____

_____

_____

_____

_____

_____

413 Detail of *Christ of the Pentecost.* Saint Madeleine Cathedral, Vézelay, France. 1125–1150. *(page 282)*

_____

_____

_____

_____

_____

_____

_____

_____

_____

_____

414a-b *Notre Dame de Chartres.* Chartres, France. 1145–1513.   a. View from the southeast. *(page 283)*   b. *West Front. (page 284)*

_____

_____

_____

_____

_____

_____

_____

_____

414c-d   c. *"Rose de France" Window.* c.
1233. *(page 284)*   d. *Old Testament Prophet,
Kings, and Queen.* c. 1145–1170. *(page 285)*

414e *e.* Plan based on Latin cross. *(page 285)*

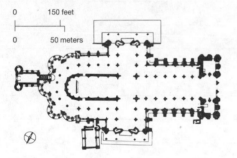

Chapter Seventeen
Renaissance
and Baroque Europe

415 Giotto di Bondone. *Lamentation.* Scrovegni Chapel, Padua, Italy. c. 1305. *(page 287)*

416 Masaccio. *The Holy Trinity.* Santa Maria Novella, Florence. 1425. *(page 288)*

417 Donatello. *David.* c. 1425–1430. *(page 289)*

418 Donatello. *Mary Magdalen.* c. 1455. *(page 289)*

419 Sandro Botticelli. *Birth of Venus.* c. 1480. *(page 290)*

420 Leonardo da Vinci (1452–1519). *The Infant and Womb.* c. 1510. *(page 291)*

421 Leonardo da Vinci. *Mona Lisa.* c. 1503–1506. *(page 291)*

422 Leonardo da Vinci. *The Last Supper.* Santa Maria delle Grazie, Milan. c. 1495–1498. *(page 292)*

422a-b a. Perspective lines as both organizing structure and symbol of content. b. Christ's figure as stable triangle, contrasting with active turmoil of the disciples. *(page 292)*

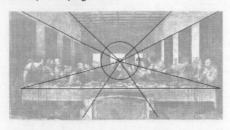

423 Leonardo da Vinci. *Self-Portrait.* c. 1512. *(page 293)*

424 Daniele da Volterra. *Michelangelo Buonarroti.* 1565. *(page 294)*

425 Michelangelo Buonarroti. a. *David*. 1501–1504. b. *David*. Close-up of head. *(page 295)*

426 Michelangelo Buonarroti. Frescoes on the ceiling and walls of *The Sistine Chapel.* Vatican, Rome. 1508–1512. a. *The Creation of Adam*, Fresco of the Sistine Chapel after restoration. b. *The Sistine Chapel* after restoration. *(page 296)*

427 Raphael. *Madonna of the Meadows*. 1505. *(page 297)*

428 Jan van Eyck. *The Marriage of Giovanni Arnolfini and Giovanna Cenami.* 1434. *(page 298)*

429 Pieter Bruegel. *The Return of the Hunters.* 1565. *(page 299)*

430 The Limbourg Brothers. *February*, from Les Très Riches Heures Du Duc de Berry. *1413–1416.* (page 299)

431 Andrea Palladio. *Villa Rotonda.* Vicenza,
Italy. 1567–1570. *(page 300)*

432 Jacopo Tintoretto. *The Last Supper.*
1592–1594. *(page 301)*

433 Michelangelo Merisi da Caravaggio. *The Conversion of Saint Paul.* 1600–1601. *(page 302)*

434 Gianlorenzo Bernini. *David.* 1623. *(page 303)*

435 Gianlorenzo Bernini. *The Ecstasy of Saint Teresa.* Detail of the altar, Cornaro Chapel, Santa Maria della Vittoria, Rome. 1645–1652. *(page 303)*

436 Peter Paul Rubens (Flemish, 1577–1640). *The Raising of the Cross.*1610–1611. *(page 304)*

437 Diego Velázquez. *The Maids of Honor.* 1656. *(page 304)*

438 Rembrandt van Rijn (1606–1669). *Return of the Prodigal Son.* c. 1668–1669. *(page 305)*

439 Rembrandt Harmensz van Rijn. *Self-Portrait Leaning on a Ledge.* 1639. *(page 306)*

440 Jan Vermeer. *The Girl With the Red Hat.* c. 1665–1666. *(page 307)*

441 Jan Vermeer. *The Kitchen Maid.* c. 1658. *(page 307)*

442 *Versailles.* c. 1665. *(page 308)*

443 Germain Boffrand. *Salon de la Princesse, Hôtel de Soubise*. Paris. Begun 1732. *(page 308)*

444 Jean Honoré Fragonard. *The Swing*. 1767. *(page 309)*

445 *Hildegard's Vision*. From *Scivias* by Hildegard of Bingen. c. 1142–1152. *(page 310)*

446 Sofonisba Anguissola (Italian, 1527–1625).
Self-Portrait. 1556. *(page 311)*

_____

_____

_____

_____

_____

_____

_____

_____

_____

_____

_____

_____

447 Artemisia Gentileschi. *Judith and the
Maidservant with the Head of Holofernes.* c. 1625.
(page 311)

_____

_____

_____

_____

_____

_____

_____

_____

_____

_____

_____

448 Michelangelo Buonarroti. *The Libyan Sibyl;*
Detail of *Sistine Chapel* ceiling frescoes, Vatican City.
a. before and b. after 1980s restoration. *(page 312)*

_____

_____

_____

_____

_____

_____

_____

_____

_____

_____

_____

449 *Uch Monument Complex.* Bahawalpur
District, Punjab Province, Pakistan. *(page 312)*

450 *Cornerstones Community Partnership.*
Hopi & Zuni youth working on restoring the
Wapatki National Monument. 1996. *(page 313)*

Chapter Eighteen
Traditional Arts of Asia

Notes

451 *Male Torso.* Harappā, Indus Valley.
c. 2400–2000 B.C.E. *(page 314)*

452 *Historical Map of Asia. (page 315)*

453 a. *Stupa I.* Sāñchī, India. 10 B.C.E.–15 C.E.
b. Eastern gate of *The Great Stupa.* (page 316)

454 *Evolution of Buddhist Architecture.* a. Early
Indian stupa. 3rd century to early 1st century
B.C.E. b. Later Indian stupa. 2nd century C.E.
c. Chinese pagoda. 5th to 7th centuries C.E.
d. Japanese pagoda. 7th century C.E. (page 316)

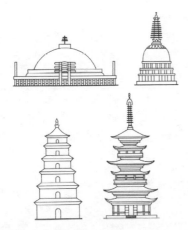

455 *Standing Bodhisattva.* N.W. Pakistan, Gandhara
region. Late 2nd century A.D. (page 317)

456 *Standing Buddha.* 5th century. *(page 318)*

457 *"Beautiful Bodhisattva" Padmapani.*
Detail of a fresco from Cave 1. Ajanta, India.
c. 600–650 *(page 318)*

458 *Kandarya Mahadeva Temple.* Khajurāho,
India. 10th–11th centuries. a. Exterior b. Scene
from *Kandariya Mahadeva Temple.* Erotic
reliefs. Chandella dynasty, 1025–50 CE.
Khajuraho, Madhya Pradesh, India. *(page 319)*

459 *Nātarāja: Shiva as King Shiva Nātarāja, Lord of the Dance.* South India, Chola Period, 11th century. *(page 320)*

460 *Radha and Krishna in the Grove.* Kangra style, c. 1780. *(page 321)*

461 *Borobudur.* Java. c. 800. a. Aerial view. *(page 322)* b. *Corridor at Borobudur.* First Gallery. *(page 322)*

462 *Angkor Wat.* c. 1120–1150. a. West
entrance. b. Plan. *(page 323)*

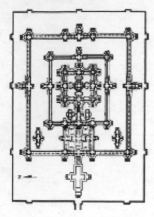

463 *Ritual Vessel (la Tigresse).* China. Shang
dynasty. c. 1100–1000 B.C.E. *(page 324)*

464 *Terra Cotta Warriors.* Pit No. 1, Museum of
the First Emperor of Qin. Shaanxi Province,
China. Han Dynasty. c. 210 B.C.E. *(page 325)*

465 *Flying Horse.* One leg resting on a swallow.
Eastern Han dynasty. 2nd century. *(page 326)*

466 *Bodhisattva Guan Yin, the Water and Moon
Guanyin Bodhisattva.* 11th–12th century Northern
Song (960–1127) or Liao Dynasty (916–1125).
Chinese, Shanxi Province. *(page 327)*

467 Huai-su. Detail of *Autobiography.* Tang
dynasty, 7th–10th centuries. *(page 328)*

468 Fan Kuan. *Travelers Among Mountains and Streams.* Song dynasty. Early 11th century. *(page 329)*

469 Wu Chen. *Album Leaf from Manual of Ink Bamboo.* 1350. *(page 330)*

470 Yu-Jian. *Mountain Village in a Mist.* 13th century. *(page 330)*

471 Tang Yin. *Whispering Pines on a Mountain Path*. Ming dynasty. c. 1516. *(page 331)*

472 *Porcelain Plate*. Mid-14th century. *(page 332)*

473 *Wine Pitcher*. Korea. Koryo dynasty. Mid-12th century. *(page 332)*

474 Bada Shanren. *Cicada on a Banana Leaf.*
Qing dynasty. 1688–1689. *(page 333)*

475 *Main Shrine.* Ise, Japan. c. 685. Rebuilt
every twenty years. *(page 334)*

476 *Horyuji Temple.* Nara, Japan. c. 670. *(page 334)*
b. Kondo, Structural diagram. *(page 335)*

477 Unkei. *Detail of Muchaku.* c. 1208. *(page 335)*

478 *Burning of the Sanjo Palace. Sanjo–Den Youchi No Emaki* (Scroll with depictions of the Night Attack on the Sanjo Palace). From the *Heiji Monogatari Emaki* (illustrated Scrolls of the Events of the Heiji Era), Japan. Second half of the 13th century. *(page 336)*

479 Sesshū, Japanese. *Haboku Landscape.* 1420–1506. *(page 337)*

480 Tawaraya Sōtatsu (Japanese, active 1600–1630).
Waves at Matsushima. 17th century. *(page 338)*

481 Utamaro Kitagawa (Japanese, 1754–1806).
*Reflected Beauty, Seven Beauties Applying
Make-up: Okita* c. 1790. *(page 338)*

482 *Katsura Detached Palace.* Kyoto, Japan.
17th century. a. Gardens and tea house.
b. Imperial gardens and villa. c. Interior of tea
house. *(page 339)*

483 Mitsutani Kunishiro. *Upstairs*. 1910.
(page 340)

Chapter Nineteen
The Islamic World

484 *Great Mosque.* Kairouan, Tunisia. 836–875. *(page 342)*

485 *Pitcher (Spouted Ewer).* Kashan. Early 13th century. *(page 342)*

486 *Text of the Koran.* North Africa or Spain.
11th century. *(page 343)*

487 *Court of the Lions, Alhambra.* Granada,
Spain. 1309–1354. *(page 343)*

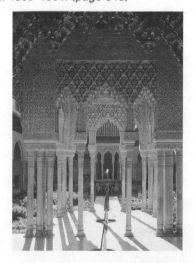

488 *The Islamic World. (page 344)*

489 *Mihrab.* Persia (Iran). c. 1354. *(page 344)*

490 *Mir-I-Arab Madrasa.* Bukhara, Uzbekistan. 1535–1536. *(page 345)*

491 Attributed to Sultan-Muhammad. *Sultan Sanjar and the Old Woman,* from the *Khamseh (Five Poems)* of Nizami, folio 181, 1539–1543. *(page 346)*

492 Mansur. *Turkey-Cock.* c. 1612. *(page 347)*

493 *Taj Mahal.* Agra, India. 1632–1648. *(page 347)*

494 Sinan. *Süleymaniye Mosque.* Istanbul, Turkey. 1550-1557. *(page 348)*

495 Sinan. *Selimiye Mosque*. Edirne, Turkey. c. 1579. *(page 348)*

Chapter Twenty
Africa, Oceania, and the Americas

496 *Africa.* (page 349)

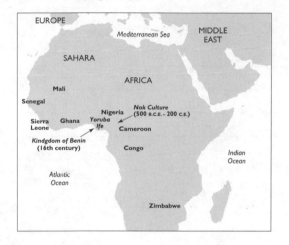

EUROPE

Mediterranean Sea

MIDDLE EAST

SAHARA

AFRICA

Mali

Senegal

Nigeria

Nok Culture (500 B.C.E. – 200 C.E.)

Sierra Leone   Ghana   *Yoruba* *Ife*   Cameroon

Kindgdom of Benin (16th century)   Congo

Atlantic Ocean

Indian Ocean

Zimbabwe

497 *Head.* Nok culture. 500 B.C.E.–200 C.E. (page 350)

498 *Male Portrait Head.* Ife, Nigeria. 12th
century. *(page 350)*

_____

_____

_____

_____

_____

_____

_____

_____

_____

_____

_____

499 *Benin Head.* Nigeria. 16th century.
(page 350)

_____

_____

_____

_____

_____

_____

_____

_____

_____

_____

_____

_____

_____

500 *Pendant Mask, Court of Benin, Portrait of
a Queen Mother.* Nigeria, Africa. Early 16th
century. *(page 351)*

_____

_____

_____

_____

_____

_____

_____

_____

_____

_____

_____

501 *Tyi Wara Dancers*. Mali. *(page 351)*

502 *Large Dance Headdress*. Bamenda area, Cameroon, Africa. 19th century. *(page 352)*

503 Olembe Alaye. *House Post*. Yoruba, Nigeria. Mid-twentieth century. *(page 352)*

504 *Tomb of Former Chief Lisa.* Ondo, Nigeria.
The *House Post* is third from left. *(page 353)*

505 *Power Figure (Nkonde).* Kongo people.
Democratic Republic of Congo, 19th–20th century.
(page 353)

506 *Gourds.* Northern Nigeria. 20th century.
(page 354)

507 *Textile (Kpokpo).* Mende peoples, Sierra Leone and Libera. *(page 354)*

508 Detail of *Adire Cloth.* Yoruba, Lagos, Nigeria. 1984. *(page 354)*

509 Kane Kwei with *Lamborghini Coffin.* 1991. *(page 355)*

510 *Oceania and Australia.* (page 356)

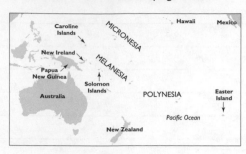

511 *Protective Prow Figure from a War Canoe.* New Georgia Island, Solomon Islands. 19th century. *(page 356)*

512 *Mask.* New Ireland. C. 1920. *(page 357)*

513 *Coconut Grater.* Kapingamarangi, Caroline Islands. 1954. *(page 357)*

514 *Standing Female Figure.* Nujuoro Atoll, Central Carolines. *(page 357)*

515 *Feather Cape.* Hawaii. 18th century. *(page 358)*

516 *Aumakua.* Wooden image from Forbes
Cave, Hawaii. *(page 358)*

517 *Maori Meeting House.* Called
"Ruatepupuke." New Zealand. 1881.
a. Front view. b. Ridge pole. *(page 359)*

518 Bunia. *Funerary Rites and Spirit's Pathway
After Death. (page 360)*

519 *Americas. (page 361)*

520 *Great Serpent Mount.* Ohio. Adena culture. 100 B.C.E.–500 C.E. *(page 361)*

521 *Hand-Shaped Cutout.* Hopewell Mound, Ohio. c. 150. *(page 361)*

522 *Blanket, Banded Background.* Navajo.
1870–1875. *(page 362)*

523 Maria Chino (USA, 1901–1973). *Water Jar.*
pre–1927. *(page 362)*

524 Marshall Lomakema. *Hopi Kachina, Humis
Katsina Figure.* 1971. *(page 363)*

525 *Pomo Feather Basket.* California. 1937.
(page 363)

526 Mato Tope (Four Bears). *Robe with Mato Tope's Exploits.* c. 1835. *(page 364)*

527 *Tlingit Community House.* Ketchikan, Alaska. *(page 364)*

528 Howling Wolf. *Classroom at Fort Marion.* 1876. *(page 365)*

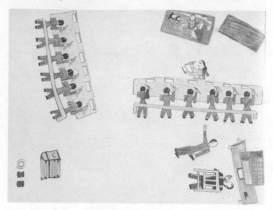

529 *Pyramid of the Sun.* Teotihuacan. 1st–7th century C.E. *(page 366)*

530 Detail of *Temple of the Feathered Serpent.* Teotihuacan. 150–200 C.E. *(page 366)*

531 *Temple I.* Maya. Tikal, Guatemala.
c. 300–900 C.E. *(page 367)*

532 *Lintel* 24. Yaxchilan, Maya. 709 C.E.
(page 367)

533 *Chacmool.* 10th–12th century. Toltec.
(page 368)

534 *Vessel of the Feathered Serpent Quetzalcoatl.* Aztec. 1450–1521. *(page 368)*

535 *Machu Picchu.* Inca. Peru. Early 16th century. *(page 369)*

536 *Hummingbird.* Nazca Valley, Peru. *(page 369)*

537 *Kero Cup.* Peru. Late 16th-17th century.
(page 369)

_____

_____

_____

_____

_____

_____

_____

_____

_____

_____

538 *Feathered Serpent and Flowering Trees.*
Probably Metepec, A.D. 650–750, Teotihuacan,
Techinantitla, Mexico. *(page 370)*

_____

_____

_____

_____

_____

_____

_____

_____

_____

_____

_____

PART SIX
The Modern World

Giacomo Balla. *Abstract Speed the Car has Passed.* 1913. *(page 371)*

Notes

_____

_____

_____

_____

_____

_____

_____

_____

_____

_____

_____

Chapter Twenty-One
Late Eighteenth and Nineteenth Centuries

Notes

539 Jacques-Louis David. *Oath of the Horatii.* *1784.* (page 373)

540 Angelica Kauffmann (born Swiss, 1741–1807). *Cornelia, Pointing to Her Children as Her Treasures.* c. 1785. (page 373)

541 Thomas Jefferson. *Monticello.*
Charlottesville, Virginia. 1793–1806. *(page 374)*

542 Francisco de Goya y Lucientes (1746–1828).
The Third of May. 1814. *(page 375)*

543 John Constable. *The Hay Wain.* 1821.
(page 376)

544 Thomas Cole. *The Oxbow.* 1836. *(page 377)*

545 Robert S. Duncanson. *Blue Hole, Little Miami River.* 1851. *(page 377)*

546 Eugène Delacroix. *The Death of Sardanapalus.* 1827. *(page 378)*

547 Carleton E. Watkins. *The Three Brothers–4480 Feet–Yosemite.* 1861. *(page 379)*

548 Nadar (Félix Tournachon). *Sarah Bernhardt.* 1855. *(page 380)*

549 Gustave Courbet (1819–1877). *The Stone Breakers.* 1849 (destroyed in 1945). *(page 381)*

550 Rosa Bonheur. *The Horse Fair.* 1853–1855. *(page 382)*

551 Rosa Bonheur. *Study for the Horse Fair.* c. 1853. *(page 382)*

552 W. H. Mote. *Rosa Bonheur.* 1856. *(page 383)*

553 Jean Léon Gérôme. *Pygmalion and Galatea.* c. 1860. *(page 384)*

554 Thomas Eakins. *William Rush Carving His Allegorical Figure of the Schuylkill River.* 1876–77. *(page 384)*

555 Henry Ossawa Tanner. *The Banjo Lesson.* 1893. *(page 385)*

556 Edouard Manet. *Luncheon on the Grass (Le Déjeuner Sur L'herbe).* 1863. *(page 386)*

557 Claude Monet. (French, 1840–1926). *On the Bank of the Seine, Bennecourt (Au Bord de L'eau, Bennecourt).* 1868. *(page 387)*

558 Claude Monet. *Impression: Sunrise.* 1872. *(page 388)*

559 *Claude Monet on His Eightieth Birthday.*
1920. *(page 389)*

560 Pierre-Auguste Renoir. *The Luncheon of the Boating Party.* 1881. *(page 390)*

561 Edgar Degas. *The Ballet Class.* c. 1879–1880.
(page 391)

562 Mary Cassatt (American, 1844–1926). *The Boating Party.* 1893–1894. *(page 392)*

563 Auguste Rodin (1840–1917). *The Thinker (Le Penseur).* c. 1910 *(page 393)*

564 Georges Seurat. *A Sunday on la Grande Jatte.* 1884–1886. *(page 394)*

565 Paul Cézanne. *Mont Sainte-Victoire.*
1902–1904. *(page 395)*

_____

_____

_____

_____

_____

_____

_____

_____

_____

566 Paul Cézanne. *Self-Portrait. (page 396)*

_____

_____

_____

_____

_____

_____

_____

_____

567 Vincent van Gogh, after Hiroshige.
Japonaiserie: Flowering Plum Tree. 1887.
(page 397)

_____

_____

_____

_____

_____

_____

_____

_____

_____

568 Vincent van Gogh. *The Sower.* 1888. *(page 397)*

_____

_____

_____

_____

_____

_____

_____

_____

_____

_____

569 Vincent van Gogh. *The Starry Night.* 1889. *(page 398)*

_____

_____

_____

_____

_____

_____

_____

_____

_____

_____

_____

570 Paul Gauguin. *The Vision After the Sermon (Jacob Wrestling with the Angel).* 1888. *(page 399)*

_____

_____

_____

_____

_____

_____

_____

_____

_____

_____

571 Paul Gauguin. (French, 1848-1903). *Fatata te Miti (By the Sea).* 1892. *(page 400)*

572 Paul Gauguin. *Portrait of the Artist with the Idol.* c. 1893. *(page 401)*

573 Henri de Toulouse-Lautrec. *At the Moulin Rouge.* 1892–1895. *(page 402)*

574 Edvard Munch. *The Shriek.* 1896.
(page 403)

_____

_____

_____

_____

_____

_____

_____

_____

_____

_____

_____

Chapter Twenty-Two
Early Twentieth Century

Notes

575 Constantin Brancusi. *Sleep.* 1908.
(page 405)

_____
_____
_____
_____
_____
_____
_____
_____
_____
_____

576 Constantin Brancusi. *Sleeping Muse.*
1909–1911. *(page 405)*

_____
_____
_____
_____
_____
_____
_____
_____
_____
_____

577 Constantin Brancusi. *The Newborn.* 1915.
(page 405)

_____

_____

_____

_____

_____

_____

_____

_____

_____

_____

578 *Cycladic II.* Female statuette. 2700–2300 B.C.E.
(page 405)

_____

_____

_____

_____

_____

_____

_____

_____

_____

_____

_____

_____

_____

579 Constantin Brancusi. *Bird in Space.* 1928.
(page 406)

_____

_____

_____

_____

_____

_____

_____

_____

_____

_____

_____

_____

Notes

580 Henri Matisse. *Le Bonheur de Vivre.*
1905–1906. *(page 408)*

---

581 André Derain. *London Bridge.* 1906.
(page 409)

---

582 Ernst Ludwig Kirchner. *Street, Berlin.* 1913.
(page 410)

---

583 Vasily Kandinsky. *Blue Mountain (Der Blaue Berg)*. 1908–1909. *(page 411)*

584 Wassily Kandinsky. *With the Black Arch No. 154*. 1912. *(page 411)*

585 Pablo Picasso. *Self-Portrait with Palette*. 1906. *(page 412)*

586 *Iberian Stone Relief. (page 412)*

587 *Bakota Funerary Figure.* French Equatorial
Africa, probably 20th century. *(page 412)*

588 *Mask from Ivory Coast. (page 412)*

589 Pablo Picasso. *Les Demoiselles D'Avignon.*
Paris, June-July 1907. *(page 413)*

590 Paul Cézanne. *Gardanne.* 1885–1886.
(page 414)

591 Georges Braque. (1882-1963) *Houses at
L'Estaque.* 1908. *(page 414)*

592 Georges Braque. *The Portuguese*. 1911.
(page 415)

_____

_____

_____

_____

_____

_____

_____

_____

_____

593 Pablo Picasso (Spanish, 1881-1973) *Violin and Fruit*. 1913. *(page 416)*

_____

_____

_____

_____

_____

_____

_____

_____

_____

_____

_____

594 Pablo Picasso. *Guitar*. Paris, winter 1912–13.
(page 416)

_____

_____

_____

_____

_____

_____

_____

_____

_____

_____

595 *Picasso in His Studio at Cannes.* c. 1965.
(page 417)

596 Alfred Stieglitz. *The Steerage.* 1907. From
Camera Work, New York, No. 34, October 1911.
(page 418)

597 Georgia O'Keeffe. *Light Coming on the
Plains No II.* 1917. *(page 418)*

598 Frank Lloyd Wright. *Robie House.* Chicago, Illinois. 1909. *(page 419)*

599 Giacomo Balla (1871-1958). *Abstract Speed-The Car Has Passed.* 1913. *(page 420)*

600 Umberto Boccioni. *Unique Forms of Continuity in Space.* 1913. *(page 420)*

601 Marcel Duchamp (American, b. France
1887–1968). *Nude Descending a Staircase,
No. 2, 1912.* (page 421)

602 Sonia Delaunay. *Bal Bullier.* 1913.
(page 421)

Chapter Twenty-Three
Between World Wars

603 Marcel Duchamp. *L.H.O.O.Q.* 1919. *(page 423)*

_____
_____
_____
_____
_____
_____
_____
_____
_____
_____

604 Man Ray. *Cadeau (The Gift).* c. 1958. *(page 425)*

_____
_____
_____
_____
_____
_____
_____
_____
_____
_____
_____

605 Raoul Hausmann. *The Spirit of Our Time.*
1919. *(page 424)*

_____

_____

_____

_____

_____

_____

_____

_____

_____

_____

606 Hannah Höch. *The Multi-Millionaire.* 1923.
(page 424)

_____

_____

_____

_____

_____

_____

_____

_____

_____

607 Paul Klee. *Twittering Machine (Zwitscher–
Maschine).* 1922. *(page 425)*

_____

_____

_____

_____

_____

_____

_____

_____

_____

608 Marc Chagall. *The Birthday (l'Anniversaire).*
1915. *(page 425)*

_____

_____

_____

_____

_____

_____

_____

_____

_____

_____

_____

609 Giorgio De Chirico. *The Mystery and
Melancholy of a Street.* 1914. *(page 426)*

_____

_____

_____

_____

_____

_____

_____

_____

_____

_____

_____

610 Salvador Dali. *The Persistence of Memory
(Persistance de la Memoire).* 1931. *(page 427)*

_____

_____

_____

_____

_____

_____

_____

_____

_____

_____

_____

_____

611 Joan Miró (Spanish 1893–1983). *Woman Haunted by the Passage of the Bird-Dragonfly Omen of Bad News.* 1938. *(page 427)*

612 René Magritte. *Portrait.* 1935. *(page 428)*

613 Frida Kahlo (1907–1954). *The Two Fridas.* 1939. *(page 428)*

614 Frida Kahlo. *The Love Embrace of the Universe, the Earth (Mexico), Diego, Me, and Señor Xolotl.* 1949. *(page 429)*

615 Fernand Léger. *The City.* 1919. *(page 430)*

616 Kasimir Malevich. *Suprematist Composition: Airplane Flying.* 1915. (dated 1914). *(page 431)*

617 Tarsila do Amaral. *Abaporu.* 1928.
(page 431)

618 Vladimir Tatlin. *Model for Monument to the Third International.* 1919–1920. *(page 432)*

619 Piet Mondrian (1872–1944). *Composition with Red, Yellow, and Blue. 1930.* (page 433)

620 Piet Mondrian. *Broadway Boogie-Woogie.*
1942–1943. *(page 433)*

621 Gerrit Rietveld. *Schröder House, Utrecht.*
1924. *(page 434)*

622 Le Corbusier. *Villa Savoye.* Poissy, France.
1928–1930. *(page 434)*

623 Max Beckmann. *Departure.* 1932–1933.
(page 435)

624 Pablo Picasso. *Guernica.* 1937. *(page 436)*

625 Vera Mukhina. *Monument to the Proletariat and Agriculture.* 1937. *(page 437)*

626 *Diego Rivera and Frida Kahlo.* c. 1930.
(page 438)

627 Diego Rivera (Mexican, 1886–1959). *The Liberation of the Peon.* 1931. *(page 439)*

628 Dorothea Lange. *White Angel Bread Line, San Francisco.* 1933. *(page 440)*

629 Edward Hopper (American, 1882–1973).
Nighthawks. 1942. *(page 440)*

630 Grant Wood (American, 1891–1942).
American Gothic. 1930. *(page 441)*

631 Thomas Hart Benton (American, 1889–1975).
Palisades, from the series *American Historical Epic.* C. 1919–1924. *(page 442)*

632 Archibald Motley, Jr. *Barbecue.* 1934. *(page 442)*

_____

_____

_____

_____

_____

_____

_____

_____

_____

_____

_____

Chapter Twenty-Four
Accelerated Change: Modern Art After 1945

Notes

633 Hans Hofmann. *Idolatress I.* 1944. *(page 444)*

634 Jackson Pollock. *Autumn Rhythm.* *(Number 30)*, 1950. *(page 444)*

238

635 Mark Rothko. *Blue, Orange, Red.* 1961.
(page 445)

_____

_____

_____

_____

_____

_____

_____

_____

_____

_____

636 Helen Frankenthaler. *Mountains and Sea.*
1952. *(page 445)*

_____

_____

_____

_____

_____

_____

_____

_____

_____

_____

_____

637 Robert Motherwell. *Elegy to the Spanish
Republic No. 34*, 1953–1954. *(page 446)*

_____

_____

_____

_____

_____

_____

_____

_____

_____

638 Willem de Kooning. *Woman and Bicycle.*
1952–1953. *(page 447)*

_____

_____

_____

_____

_____

_____

_____

_____

_____

_____

_____

_____

639 Norman Lewis. (1909-1979). *Untitled.* c.
1947. *(page 447)*

_____

_____

_____

_____

_____

_____

_____

_____

_____

_____

_____

_____

_____

_____

640 Asger Jorn. *The Great Victory.* 1955–1956.
(page 448)

_____

_____

_____

_____

_____

_____

_____

_____

_____

_____

_____

_____

_____

641 Alberto Burri. (b. 1915). *Sacking and Red,* 1954. *(page 448)*

_____

_____

_____

_____

_____

_____

_____

_____

_____

_____

642 David Smith. *Cubi XVII.* 1963. *(page 449)*

_____

_____

_____

_____

_____

_____

_____

_____

_____

_____

_____

_____

643 Harry Callahan. (American, b. 1912). *Multiple Trees.* 1949. *(page 449)*

_____

_____

_____

_____

_____

_____

_____

_____

_____

_____

644 Robert Louis Frank (American, b. 1924).
Trolley, New Orleans. From *The Americans.*
(page 450)

645 Skidmore, Owings, and Merrill. *Lever
House.* 1952. *(page 450)*

646 Robert Rauschenberg. *Monogram.*
1955–1959. *(page 451)*

647 Robert Rauschenberg. *Canyon.* 1959.
(page 451)

_____

_____

_____

_____

_____

_____

_____

_____

_____

_____

648 Robert Rauschenberg (American, born
1925). *Tracer.* 1963. *(page 452)*

_____

_____

_____

_____

_____

_____

_____

_____

_____

_____

_____

649 *Robert Rauschenberg. (page 452)*

_____

_____

_____

_____

_____

_____

_____

_____

_____

_____

650 Jasper Johns, *Target with Four Faces.*
1955. *(page 453)*

_____
_____
_____
_____
_____
_____
_____
_____
_____
_____
_____
_____
_____

651 Niki de Saint Phalle. *St. Sebastien, or the
Portrait of My Love.* 1960. *(page 453)*

_____
_____
_____
_____
_____
_____
_____
_____
_____
_____
_____
_____

652 Jean Tinguely. *Homage to New York: A
Self-Constructing, Self-Destructing Work of Art.*
1960. *(page 454)*

_____
_____
_____
_____
_____
_____
_____
_____
_____
_____
_____
_____

653 Allan Kaprow. *Household.* Happening commissioned by Cornell University, performed May 1964. *(page 455)*

654 Richard Hamilton, (English, b. 1922). *Just What Is It That Makes Today's Homes So Different, So Appealing?* 1959. *(page 456)*

655 James Rosenquist. *F-111.* 1965. *(page 457)*

656 Andy Warhol. *Marilyn Diptych.* 1962.
(page 457)

_____

_____

_____

_____

_____

_____

_____

_____

_____

_____

_____

657 Roy Lichtenstein. *Drowning Girl.* 1963.
(page 458)

_____

_____

_____

_____

_____

_____

_____

_____

_____

_____

_____

_____

658 Claes Oldenburg. *Two Cheeseburgers with
Everything (Dual Hamburgers).* 1962. *(page 458)*

_____

_____

_____

_____

_____

_____

_____

_____

_____

_____

_____

659 Donald Judd. *Untitled.* 1967. *(page 459)*

_____

_____

_____

_____

_____

_____

_____

_____

_____

_____

660 Ellsworth Kelly. *Blue, Green, Yellow, Orange, Red.* 1966. *(page 460)*

_____

_____

_____

_____

_____

_____

_____

_____

_____

_____

661 Frank Stella. (American, b. 1936). *Agbatana III.* 1968. *(page 460)*

_____

_____

_____

_____

_____

_____

_____

_____

_____

_____

_____

662 Joseph Kosuth. *One and Three Chairs.*
1965. *(page 461)*

663 Christo and Jeanne–Claude. *Running Fence.* Sonoma and Marin Counties, California. 1972–1976. *(page 462)*

664 Walter De Maria. *The Lightning Field.* Quemado, New Mexico. 1977. *(page 462)*

665 Robert Smithson. *Spiral Jetty.* Great Salt Lake, Utah. 1970. *(page 463)*

_____
_____
_____
_____
_____
_____
_____
_____
_____
_____

666 James Turrell. *Amba.* 1982. *(page 464)*

_____
_____
_____
_____
_____
_____
_____
_____
_____
_____
_____

667 Red Grooms and the Ruckus Construction Company. *Ruckus Manhattan.* 1976. *(page 465)*

_____
_____
_____
_____
_____
_____
_____
_____
_____
_____
_____

668 Judy Chicago. *The Dinner Party.* 1979.
(page 466)

_____

_____

_____

_____

_____

_____

_____

_____

_____

_____

_____

_____

669 Nancy Spero. *Rebirth of Venus.* Detail. 1984.
(page 467)

_____

_____

_____

_____

_____

_____

_____

_____

_____

_____

_____

_____

670 Louise Bourgeois. *The Destruction of the
Father.* 1974. *(page 467)*

_____

_____

_____

_____

_____

_____

_____

_____

_____

_____

_____

_____

671 Joseph Beuys. *I Like America and America Likes Me.* 1974. *(page 468)*

_____

_____

_____

_____

_____

_____

_____

_____

_____

_____

672 Ana Mendieta. *Tree of Life Series.* 1977. *(page 468)*

_____

_____

_____

_____

_____

_____

_____

_____

_____

_____

_____

_____

_____

673 Mierle Laderman Ukeles. *A.I.R. Wash.* 1973. *(page 469)*

_____

_____

_____

_____

_____

_____

_____

_____

_____

_____

_____

_____

674 Richard Estes. *Horn and Hardart Automat.*
1967. *(page 470)*

_____

_____

_____

_____

_____

_____

_____

_____

_____

_____

_____

675 Duane Hanson. *Tourists.* 1970. *(page 470)*

_____

_____

_____

_____

_____

_____

_____

_____

_____

_____

_____

_____

676 Katsukawa Shunsho. *Iwai Hanshiro IV as
Mistress of Soga-No-Juro.* 1792. *(page 471)*

_____

_____

_____

_____

_____

_____

_____

_____

_____

_____

_____

_____

677 Xu Bing. *A Book from the Sky.* 1987–1991.
Museo Nacional Centro de Arte Reina Sofia,
Madrid, Spain. *(page 471)*

678 Chris Ofili. *The Holy Virgin Mary.* 1996.
(page 472)

Chapter Twenty-Five
Recent Diversity

Notes

679 Johnson and Burgee. *A.T.&T. Building.*
New York City. 1978–1984. *(page 474)*

680 Michael Graves. *Public Services Building.*
Portland, Oregon. 1980–1982. *(page 475)*

681 Arata Isozaki. *Team Disney Building.*
Orlando, Florida. 1990. *(page 475)*

682 Susan Rothenberg (American, 1945–). *Blue Head.* 1980–1981. *(page 475)*

683 Eric Fischl. *Untitled.* 1986. *(page 476)*

684 Anselm Kiefer. *Osiris and Isis.* 1985–1987.
(page 477)

_____

_____

_____

_____

_____

_____

_____

_____

_____

_____

_____

_____

685 Elizabeth Murray. *More Than You Know.*
1983. *(page 478)*

_____

_____

_____

_____

_____

_____

_____

_____

_____

_____

_____

_____

686 Kerry James Marshall. *Better Homes
Better Gardens.* 1994. *(page 478)*

_____

_____

_____

_____

_____

_____

_____

_____

_____

_____

_____

_____

687 Sarah Charlesworth. *Still Life with Camera.*
1995. *(page 479)*

_____

_____

_____

_____

_____

_____

_____

_____

_____

_____

_____

_____

688 Sandy Skoglund. *Revenge of the Goldfish.*
1981. *(page 480)*

_____

_____

_____

_____

_____

_____

_____

_____

_____

_____

_____

689 Cindy Sherman. *Untitled Film Still.* 1979.
(page 480)

_____

_____

_____

_____

_____

_____

_____

_____

_____

_____

_____

690 Martin Puryear. *Old Mole.* 1985. *(page 481)*

_____

_____

_____

_____

_____

_____

_____

_____

_____

_____

_____

691 Anish Kapoor. *To Reflect an Intimate Part of the Red.* 1981. *(page 482)*

_____

_____

_____

_____

_____

_____

_____

_____

_____

_____

_____

_____

_____

692 Kiki Smith. *Ice Man.* 1995. *(page 482)*

_____

_____

_____

_____

_____

_____

_____

_____

_____

_____

_____

_____

_____

693 Maya Lin. *Vietnam Veterans Memorial.* The Mall, Washington, D.C. 1980–1982. *(page 484)*

694 Frederick Hart. *Vietnam Memorial Sculpture.* The Mall, Washington, D.C. 1984. *(page 484)*

695 R. M. Fischer. *Rector Gate.* 1988. *(page 485)*

696 Mierle Laderman Ukeles. *The Social Mirror.* New York. 1983. *(page 486)*

697 Mierle Laderman Ukeles with New York City Department of Sanitation. *Landfill Cross Section.* 1990. *(page 486)*

698 Richard Misrach. *Submerged Lamppost, Salton Sea.* 1985. *(page 487)*

699 Barbara Kruger. *Untitled (I Shop Therefore I Am).* 1987. *(page 487)*

700 Fred Wilson. *Mining the Museum.* 1992. *(page 488)*

701 Cildo Meireles. *Olvido (Oblivion).* 1987–89. *(page 488)*

702 William Kentridge. Drawing from *History of the Main Complaint.* (Title Page). 1996. *(page 489)*

703 Jaune Quick-to-See Smith. *Petroglyph Park.* 1986. *(page 489)*

704 Masami Teraoka. *Geisha and AIDS Nightmare* from the *AIDS Series.* 1989–1990. *(page 490)*

705 Fodé Camara. *Parcours–Tricolore II.* 1988. *(page 491)*

706 Ravinder G. Reddy. *Woman with Lotus Flower.* 1998. *(page 491)*

707 Tunga. *Palindromo Incesto.* 1994. *(page 492)*

708 Cai Guo Qiang. *Cultural Melting Bath: Projects for the Twentieth Century.* 1997. *(page 493)*

709 Zaha Hadid. *Cincinnati Contemporary Art Center.* Presentation Model, 1998. *(page 493)*

710 Fritz Koenig. *Sphere for Plaza Foundation.* a. damaged.   b. repaired and reinstalled. *(page 494)*